Design
Space

Crafts Now

CONTENTS

Introduction

Now after reading and understanding the features and functions of Cricut machine, we talk about the "Design Space" which is a company app for building projects and getting your output or results just like a printer. "Design Space" for Cricut machine is just like as "Windows Operating System" which run the Computer system, Cricut machine work on the instructions of the "Design space". You can use "Design Space" without Cricut machine, but you can't use Cricut Joy, Cricut Maker, and Cricut Explore family machines without "Design space". Remember that we are not talking about Easypress and Cuttlebug Cricut they don't work with any design space, as we've talked about them in our first book chapter Cricut Models.

Design space is one software for all type of Cricut machines, you're crafting and DIY project (Cricut Joy, Cricut Maker, and Cricut Explore family, need to select your device later we will talk about its selection). "Design Space" application is developed to let the artist inside you flourish into the world of technological advancements or even if you're not an artist by birth but can act as an artist with virtual artistic abilities. It is free and easy-to-learn software. It is a cloud-based application, and its new desktop software has the feature to save your project on the computer. Its cloud-based system allows you to seamlessly access all your design files from any device whenever you need it.

The Cricut Design Space, maybe quite mystifying and irritating for you as a beginner at first look because there are too many tools and functions to work. Perhaps you have decided to buy a Cricut Machine, and want to learn, how it'll function and make designs. Maybe you aren't a newbie in Cricut working but still practicing how to use the latest features of Design Space, it seems to be getting more complicated than ever. Maybe you're someone who bought Cricut for starting a small business but need a proper guideline for understanding its fundamentals. Regardless of the reasons, it would be best if you had help and guidance to become friend of it from its starting to latest features, you are reading the right book to learn the Cricut family. The reason for writing this book is to make things easier for all users.

Maybe you have read books about Cricut but not about Design Space and projects because writer talking about Cricut models, not about its application and project this incomplete knowledge and learning force you to buy another separate book for Design Space but you can't. The beauty of this bundle is that you have all three meaningful understanding in one place.

This book will increase your knowledge about Design Space of "How to correctly use new features" after updating because the company has shut down Design Space for Web on September 29, 2020. Now after September 20 all-new Design Space is available for Desktop app, Mac, and Windows computer. This book will give you a lot of insights into how you download its software and run on the system. Reading this book helps you clearly articulate how you work with ANY material. The knowledge you gain from reading this book also gives you lots to do your project on other designing apps like adobe, Canva, word or PowerPoint, save them in PDF and upload on Design Space.

In the chapters of this book, we will discuss the basic features of the Cricut Explore family devices, Cricut Joy, and Cricut Maker all three in one book. The main reason for talking about all three is that Design Space is essential for all of the Cricut, as mentioned above devices. Our focus is giving information on the family of Cricut at one place. The Canvas overview will focus on in parts that can be enabled with the Cricut Explore family, Cricut Joy and Cricut Maker. In the first chapter of this book, you will learn everything about the different kinds of Cricut Explore machines, Cricut Joy and Cricut Maker that you could purchase for yourself, along with its current prices and information available in the market or not. In chapter no 2 "How to start" will guide you what first steps take to start working. Step by step instruction given to install the Design Space in your Devices whether is it Desktop or Android Mobile or IOS system. Even guide you on how to sign up in Cricut family for getting access to its Cricut library. Chapter No 3 is essential and pillar of this book "Design Space for beginners", because we say we are guiding beginners, so we write to heart teach you every single design space tool in simple English with the help of pictures. There is a detailed overview of the Design Space application canvas with screenshots provided so you can understand the use of every tool on the canvas area, so quickly start your crafting journey. In this, we also tell you how you can use the Cricut ready-made projects, make changes in it and create a new one from it.

This chapter is all about Cricut canvas so we tell you in steps how you can use shapes from in the Cricut and place them in layers to create a new one. What the layers are and how to play with them. Is it permitted to work only with the Cricut's own tools, fonts, images and projects? Do you like any image from outside the Cricut library? Do you make your own image in PowerPoint or Word, or Adobe or even with Canva? But the question comes in mind can I use these images within my Cricut machine ground to get a Print, Cut, Score, wave or draw whatever? Don't be too hurry! Chapter 4 is all about image uploading, convert image from single layer to multiple layers, edit them on the Canvas and make them ready to "Make It". In this chapter, we also guide you on how to download third party font and use them in Cricut. The final chapter 5 is giving you some directions and ideas about how to make text effects with images.

When working with Cricut machine, there always new and better updates that are happening to the machine, so now is the best time to get one and get in the door to understanding what all it can do for you. We hope that the information we have provided you on what materials you can use with the machine, how to get your first project started, and all the project ideas are the tools you need to achieve the goals that you have with the Cricut machine.

If at any point, you get stumped on how to use your machine or are wondering what materials you should use, reference the book or visit the Cricut website for help. Understanding and studying the foundations of your Cricut is wise to make sure you are building on your skills with a solid foundation of knowledge. From there, your creativity can blossom, and the sky is the limit for what you can create. I hope that you will enjoy this book and learned a lot!

1 Chapter

Cricut Family

As we talk before Design Space is an app where you can design your own project, cut wirelessly and can use already stored projects with Cricut Explore, Cricut Maker, and Cricut Joy.

Anything for the beginners can be complicated if they can't access the right person for guidance and machine for working. For the newbies, access to the suitable crafting machine for DIYING objects can help them to convert their initial ideas into creative plots, and confidently cut project ideas that they think unachievable or impractical.

The word "Cricut" which sounds as like invites people to play and cut have increasingly been established as cutting plotters, or computer-controlled cutting machines, for home crafters. But the company's continuously ongoing efforts to widen the speed and accuracy to cut a wider variety of craft material and cutting materials list also going on to increase after every experiment.

From the first Cricut machine launched by Cricut in its limited properties to the latest model of the Cricut Joy, which is capable of cutting up to 20 feet, the Cricut Company has helped a lot to convert crafting ideas into creations. An overview of the various Cricut cutting machines has been provided in the first part of this three-book series called "Cricut for Beginners." This book will focus primarily on the Cricut Explore family, Cricut Maker and Cricut Joy. After reading this electronic die-cutting machine introduction and features, you will be in the position to make the right decision which Cricut model is best for your project so you won't be kicking yourself in the future about your decision. Down below we first discuss some properties of the Cricut Machines.

Properties:

- With it, you can Design and cut DIY projects with the cutting machines Cricut Explore, Cricut Maker, and Cricut Joy.
- Cricut Explore & Cricut Maker machines can cut so many

materials and its team postulate that the only limit is our "imagination", but it can't cut fondant or similar materials. So, don't try cutting of such materials with these two machines because it's not safe for food.

- Cricut Joy works with vinyl, cardstock, iron-on, paper – even materials you already have at home like construction paper. Cricut Joy works with IOS App and also on the desktop.
- There are 100,000+ Cricut Images, 100's of fonts and projects in the design space image library. Or you can also upload your own pictures edit them with design space features to take your projects to the next level.
- Use ready-made saved projects quickly and easily.
- Design your home and party, business cards and invitations, dress and jewelry, bags and shoes, caps and socks, children's craft, schools and classrooms, and the list goes on.
- Sign up from Cricut.com to save your images and projects on cloud and access from any device. Quickly buy a subscription from Cricut.com or Design Space.
- Use Bluetooth wireless to send projects wirelessly to the Cricut Machines.
- Its desktop software allows user to download pictures and fonts on devices so the user can continue designing and cutting project without internet and WIFI connection.

There is a total of three current Cricut cutting machine models available in the Cricut shop. For helping you to make a clear decision which model you should buy we inform you that Legacy machines, Cricut Gypsy, Cricut Cake, Cricut Personal, Cricut Expression, and the Cricut Expression 2 aren't being sold and supported by Cricut anymore. The original Cricut Explore, Cricut Explore One, and Cricut Explore Air are also included in them. However, these three Explore machines are still supported by Cricut and work with the current version of the Cricut Design Space desktop App. One another different type of machine Cuttlebug, which was mainly for die-cutting and embossing was also discontinued in 2019.

Cricut Explore One

The Cricut Explore One was a member of Cricut Explore Family, and it was launched on May 6, 2015. The company marketed it as its most affordable entry point into the world of precision crafting. Cricut Explore One was the most basic and best just for cutting but currently, this machine is no longer available from Cricut and not available on the Amazon and Walmart too. But it's ok if you still have your old Cricut Explore One then don't worry it still working with design space current desktop software. It had all of the precise cutting, writing, and scoring capabilities of the Explore Air machines and you could cut over 100 different materials, including vinyl, cardstock, and iron-on. It has one clamp head which cut, score and writes as shown in the picture below. Because of its one clamp head or single tool holder, it cut & write (or cut & score) in 2 steps.

It was preinstalled with premium fine point blade and housing and were compatible with a scoring stylus, deep point blade, and a variety of other tools that were bought separately. It was also consistent with Cricut Cartridges and also accessed through the Design Space application, and still, you can use them with desktop App. It was not Bluetooth-enabled meaning for wireless connectivity Cricut Explore Wireless Bluetooth Adapter was available separately, which is still available in the market. So, if you have your Mother's Cricut machine in your house, you can connect it with your Bluetooth adapter to transfer your design to the Cricut Explore One. This Bluetooth adapter cost is $25 on cricut.com shop and $27.99 on Amazon. Just to remind you, this Cricut model is retired now, so if you are looking to buy a new Cricut machine, this model is not available in Cricut, Amazon and Walmart markets.

Cricut Explore Air

The biggest differences between the Cricut Explore One and Cricut Explore Air are the mode of connectivity and two clamp head. Unlike the Cricut Explore One, the Cricut Explore Air works with a dual carriage for cutting and writing or cutting and scoring in one step. It doesn't need a separate Bluetooth adapter like Explore One because it has built-in Bluetooth connectivity. The Explore Air is same in price with Explore one but with so many more features and comes with pen, bag and accessory adapter. Its built-in Bluetooth makes it much more portable, without the tangles of endless wiring. A variety of image file formats are supported, such as SVG, JPG, PNG, BMP, GIF, and DXF. This model comes installed with the premium fine point blade and housing. This model is also not available by the Cricut brand. In short, in 2020 the Explore Air and Explore one both has emerged in Explore Air 2.

Cricut Explore Air 2

It's an updated member of Explore family with 2x speed. This is the only model which is sold and supported by Cricut. As a crafter who works on many complicated projects, Cricut Explore Air 2 is the best and most sales product of the Cricut shop. It also best for those who want to buy a Cricut machine for starting a side craft hustle. This model is in $249.99 with flawlessly cut over 100+ different types of materials including premium vinyl, iron-on and htv vinyl, cardstock, faux leather, adhesive foils, specialty paper, poster board and more. Each machine is available with a Cricut Premium Fine Point Blade and Housing, a Cricut 12-inch x12 inch Light Grip Adhesive Cutting Mat perfect for vinyl and htv projects, a Cricut Black Fine Point Pen, Cricut's Design Space app, and with a 30 days free trial to "Cricut Access".

It is available for purchase in 3 exciting colors, namely Mint Blue, Rose Anna, and Giffin Lilac. It can be used for making custom stickers, personalized home decor, home-made gifts and party favors, unique greeting cards, and more. According to the company, this DIY speed machine combines time-saving performance and class-leading simplicity. This model also has two clamp head which helps you keep the cutting blades and crafts pen ready to use and has a built-in Bluetooth connectivity. You can connect any of your devices like laptops, tablets, and phones with its built-in Bluetooth, so you don't have to deal with cables.

Cricut Maker

The Cricut company had launched a brand-new line of products designed Machine "Cricut Maker" on 20 August 2017. The purpose of this machine is cutting thicker materials like balsa wood, basswood, non-bonded fabric, and leather. Only "Cricut Maker" offers a unique technology that allows control on the direction of the blade and the cutting pressure that is best suited for the desired material. Cricut Maker is free to make virtually any DIY project, from 3D art to home decor, jewelry, iron-on, vinyl, paper projects, and so much more. Moreover, it has 10 times more cutting energy which allows you to cut thicker materials than ever before. "Cricut Maker" has been thoughtfully designed to simplify further and enhance your "DIY" experience and now offers more built-in storage to keep your tools and accessories organized and easily accessible. It is also equipped with a docking port for your mobile devices and tablets, along with a USB port so you can recharge your devices as you use it to bring your creativity to life. The "Cricut Maker" is the first and only device from "Cricut" that can be used with a "Rotary blade" to cut fabrics directly. It is also equipped with a "scoring wheel" that can exert varying pressure to allow scoring of thicker papers. It provides the most diverse variety of tools.

Those who want to work with basswood, fabric, balsa wood or non-bonded fabric Cricut Maker is the best and most updated machine. By purchasing this machine, you can start your own business by making fabric flowers—online sell your fabric cutting material for making applique designs on dress. Cut alphabets in different fonts sell them as a key chain, or home door decoration, or as a hanging decoration. This model is in $399.99, with flawlessly cut over 300+ different types of materials, 50 ready-to-make projects, and 25 digital sewing patterns. This model also has two clamp head which helps you keep the cutting blades and crafts pen ready to use and has a built-in Bluetooth connectivity. You can connect any of your devices like laptops, tablets, and phones with its built-in Bluetooth, so you don't have to deal with cables further any more.

Cricut Joy

Cricut released its cute new cutting machine on March 1st, 2020! that's not the most important thing, but you won't deny that this cool teal color looks perfect to be in a scrap room.

Well, aside from being Cricut's new mini cutting plotter, the Cricut Joy draws and cuts like its older sisters, but in a super small size that you can take anywhere.

Like the Explore Air 2 and the Maker Joy also has built-in Bluetooth. Connect Cricut Joy wirelessly to your computer, phone, or tablet and dip your toe into DIY.

The new Cricut Joy can cut image up to 4.5 inches wide and 4 feet long and can repeated cuts up to 20 feet long!!! More than the Cameo! And yes, it cuts it without a mat! So, we now have a Cricut that cuts without a mat.

This tech is compact and sleek with the size of 8.5" wide, 5" deep and 5" tall. The weight and its design are so comfortable to fit seamlessly into anywhere at home.

This tech is designed to cut, write and is easy to set up and use. With Cricut Joy, there is no excuse to personalizing, customizing, and organizing your items every time.

The Cricut Joy helps in cutting vinyl decals for walls and bottles, making labels for offices and kitchens and can cut 50+materials. Not only can these but also be used to cut out custom cards and birthday banners. The Cricut Joy is compatible just like other Cricut family with Cricut Smart materials, cuts iron-on, cardstock, and paper and even works with materials you already have at home. Works offline and comes with 50 free online projects. This model is in $179.99. You can't only take for starting a business, but it can be used with Maker or Explore for Extra help in cutting and writing up to 20 feet long.

2 Chapter

How To Start?

Imagine having a Bike and not a patrol to drive it or, worse still, having a Smartphone and not an internet connection! A waste, right? Exactly! That is how a Cricut is without the Cricut design space program! If you also do not know how to use this software, your Cricut will sit idly on your crafting table, and thinking why you place him idle.

What Exactly Is Cricut Design Space?

It allows you to create, organize, and then serve as a layout for your imaginative designs. From there, you get to import it to your Cricut devices for cutting. This software is free and is available on smartphones, Windows, and MAC. Here, you get to execute the most crucial process of plotting your design, which involves laying out that beautiful.

The design space is not your bike to drive, but the bike (Cricut machine) can't go without it. It creates space for your crafting or design on your smart devices which you want to use with as a source for Cricut Machine. By using its cloud system, you can access your account from any device and download your project for offline usage.

Now if you have your machine, whether it's an Air 2, Maker or Joy, then let's start to take the second step which is essential for Cricut. Design space about which you read in the above paragraph of "What is Design space?" If you understand its importance to take the first step.

What comes with Machine?

First time machine comes with everything which you will need to get set up and create the sample project. A free trial of Cricut Access will automatically be activated when you complete the new machine setup (which will we do in after some points).

1. If you are opening your New buying machine the first time, then what you have inside the Box. The **Explore Air 2** come with, Power Cord, USB Cord, Blade and housing (pre-installed), Quick Start Guide, 12 x 12 Standard Grip or Light Grip cutting mat, Materials for the first project, and Pen and accessory adapter (adapter pre-installed). In the Cricut, store Accessories will be bought separately. But you can check on another website too, like Amazon.

2. **Cricut Maker** machine has a USB cable, Rotary Blade with Drive Housing, Premium Fine-Point Blade with pre-installed Housing in the B

clamp. Fine-Point Pen, LightGrip™ Mat 12" x 12", FabricGrip™ Mat 12" x 12", Welcome book, Power adapter, and Materials for your first project.

3. **Cricut Joy** machine boxing has Blade with housing. Black 0.4 mm Fine Point Pen, Power adapter, StandardGrip Mat, 4.5" x 6.5", 50 ready-to-make projects online, Welcome card, Free 30-day trial membership to Cricut Access (for new subscribers) Materials for a practice a cut.

Note: If you want to purchase the Cricut Access, then visit cricut.com. Access purchasing through desktop App is available only in 4 Countries. Other countries users can buy it by IOS App or by Android.

Set Up Machine

Now, before taking an overview of Design Space. Set up your Machine.

So, if you buy Cricut machine first time or plan to, but it or even you have your mother's Cricut machine and now want to play it with your creative ideas, this is awesome.

But how will you use a Cricut machine? Well, that's what you want to find out. If puzzles of Cricut machine makes you feel confused, how to arrange, and want to know the names of tools inside the box then continue reading - here, we'll tell you how to connect your new Cricut machine and where to start first.

Step 1

First, for setting up the Cricut machine create a space for it. Like a small crafting room will be the best place for this, but it's not necessary, you can set it up in a dining room or on a study table. The important thing is an outlet nearby to the plug-in machine.

Step 2

Second, take a look at the manual and read the instructions. Often, people jump right in, without checking booklet and begin using the equipment, and this tedious for them. The best thing to do is to read all the materials you get with your machine. I also guide you in this book, if you're still stumped.

Step 3

Make sure have free space around the machine, because loading mats in and out, need a little bit space.

Step 4

The next thing to set up is, of course, the device where the Design Space will be downloaded, and designs will be created. Make sure that whatever medium you're using has an internet connection because first-time registration will be done through the internet, after download your project, and you can turn it off. If your machine does not have Bluetooth system, you will need to be plugged in directly, but if it's a wireless machine like the Air 2, Maker and Joy you can link this up to your computer.

Step 5

For machine, setup plugs in the device and power it on.

Connect the machine to your computer with the USB cord or pair it via Bluetooth.

Step 6

So, for using Cricut machines next important thing which you need is Cricut Design Spaces software, and you'll need to make sure that you have this downloaded and installed, before starting designing. Download the app if you plan to use an Android smartphone or tablet, or iPhone or iPad. Or if you're on the computer, then follow the steps given below.

How to Download Cricut Design Space for Desktop

1. Go to your browsing page and enter design.cricut.com.

2. Click on the download

3. Click below on your browsing page. Click on the downloaded file and select open.

    Or

    Open your location where you download Design Space software in the Desktop. Run it to install and wait until installation completed.

    See in the screenshots below.

4. Your desktop Cricut Design Space will start. Now you need to sign in by clicking on sign in. If you have Cricut Account ID simply sign in by adding your ID and Password.

But If you don't have ID then by clicking on Sing in, a new page will open. Where you can see an option of "Create a Cricut ID".

5. Click "Create a Cricut ID", a new page will open, enter your "First Name", "Last Name", and "Country".

First Name

Last Name

Country ▼

6. Enter your Any Email address which you already

Email / Cricut ID

Email / Cricut ID

Retype Email / Cricut ID

Password

have from other email providers (salin@gmail.com or salin@yahoo.com, or salin@hotmail.com) or you can enter your social media ID.

7.   Now check the boxes to agree with their policy and getting latest sales notifications in your Email.

    ☑ I agree to the Cricut Terms of Use and Privacy Policy

    ☑ Get DIY inspo, exclusive sales & more delivered to your inbox.

8.   Now finally click on the "Create a Cricut ID".

              [Create a Cricut ID]

9.   A new page will open. Now click on the "Next".

10.   F

low the instructions and choose your machine from three options.

11. For this Example, I choose Cricut Explore Family. The new page opening will show your selected machine. As shown in picture.

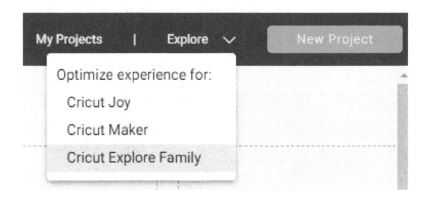

Note: Cricut Explore Family is compatible with all type of Explore Machines. It's not matter you have Explore, Explore Air, Explore Air One or Air 2.

12. Remember, if you want to change your machine at any time, all you have to do is click on the "Explore" and you will see the drop-down option for the three machines again, as you can see in the picture below.

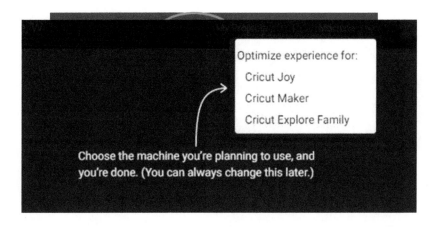

How to download Design Space on Android

You can also download and install Design Space version 3.11.3 on your Android device from the play store rather than through the web browser.

Now follow the steps for downloading the app if you want to connect your mobile with your machine.

1. Tap on the Play Store icon on your device home screen to open the Play Store.

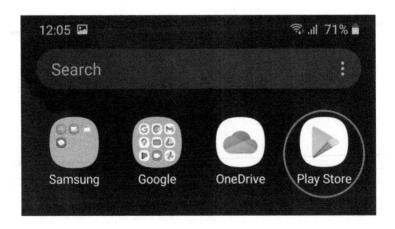

2. Search for Cricut Design Space. The Cricut Design Space app appears with its logo.

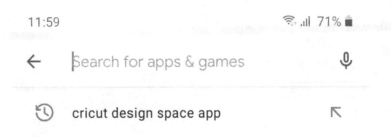

3. Tap the Install button, download it and install the app.

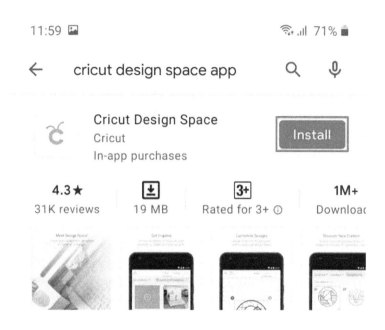

4. Once the installation complete, the app will appear on your App Home Screen. Tap on the icon, sign in, select your machine and start designing.

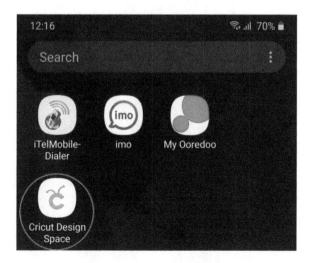

Note: Follow the same steps for downloading app in iOS device.

3 Chapter

Canvas Overview

Learning Cricut Design Space functions and features will help you to create even better crafts. Knowing how to use your Canvas and use it at its full potential will help you unleash your creativity.

Experts say that creativity needs space where creative ideas can be drawn, and Design space provides a space in the shape of canvas to its users.

The Cricut Design Space **Canvas Area** is where all of the magic happens before you cut your projects. In the space, not only you can use it for creating your design, but you can upload your fonts and images, and also use Cricut's premium images and fonts via individual purchases, Cricut Access, and Cartridges. Using a Cricut machine is just one part of your creative process. You can make something beautiful with your designer canvas to inspired people by your work and impressed them with your skills.

Investing in a Cricut is futile if you don't learn how to use Design Space and become master because you will always need this software to cut any project.

Cricut Design Space is an essential tool for Cricut cutting, drawing, and designing. And don't think that you have no experience with any other Design programs like Photoshop or Illustrator so you can't handle it. However, icons on the sides of Canvas looks overwhelming, but it is relatively easy.

You guys can Rock, if I'm non-creative person can do it, why your mind can't!

On the other hand, those users who have preview experience with any of the Adobe Creative Cloud apps. You will see that this program is just a breeze. Design Space is mainly to touch up your creative ideas and create minimal designs with Shapes and Fonts.

If you want something more sophisticated in fonts and already-make pro projects, then you need Cricut Access membership where you get access to the Cricut supergiant library. When you log into your Cricut account and want to start or edit a new project, where you will work on the Design Space is called Canvas.

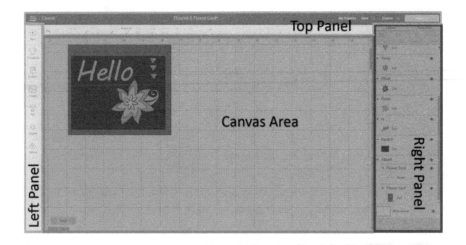

To keep everything easy for your understanding, I divided the canvas into four boxes with four colors:

1. Top Panel Green – Editing Area
2. Left Panel Orange – Insert Area
3. Right Panel Blue – Layers Area
4. Area Red - Canvas

Top Panel Green - Editing Area

The Top panel further has two Bars.

- Title Bar
- Tool Bar or Edit Bar

Title Bar

1. Three lines shows the **Main Menu** of the Design Space. This is not a part of Canvas, but it is for managing the Design Space account and whole Design Space software.
2. Canvas which shows the name of the Page currently where you are.
3. Shows the Name of the project with you are working. By default,

every new project has the title **"Untitled"**. You can rename it by clicking on the "Save" option next to the "My Projects". If you are using any readymade project, then by clicking on it, you will further go into properties of that project.

4. The Next category is **"My project"**. By clicking on "My Projects", you can redirect your library of projects you have already created. This is great because sometimes you might only want to make some changes in the previously created project. So, there no need for you to create a new one again and again.

5. **Save** option is for saving your project after every editing. This option only activates after when you place one element on canvas area. By first time clicking, you can rename your project, and after that, it will show the sub-options "Save", "Save as". Save option is used for saving any changes in the previous file, but if you want to save changes of the project with another name then by clicking on "Save as" you can add a new name.

6. Next option shows the name of the **machine** which you have to choose for cutting. You can change your device at any time by clicking on that option, but keep in mind that those tools which are working with Maker not available on Explore or Joy. So, if you have a Cricut Joy Machine and you are designing with the Maker option "ON" you won't be able to activate the tools that are for the Joy.

7. And the last one on the "Title Bar" is **"Make it"**. You have finalized your project and now if you are ready to cut then click on it for cutting.

1. Tool Bar or Image Edit Bar

This Bar is handy for editing. This Design Space bar gives you access to features such as Shape, resizes images, Arrange, Rotate, Mirror, Position, etc. Here you can choose Font for the text you'd like to use and also gives additional options like line Spacing, Letter spacing, Align designs, and more.

1.1. Undo\Redo

This toolbar feature is a standard tool in many programs. Sometimes while we work, we make mistakes. By Undo, you can perform previous actions or Redo actions means which have been undone. These little buttons are an excellent way for getting back the intricate design which you have deleted by mistake. So, in short, Undo means go back, and Redo standards do what you did Undo.

1.2. Linetype

This option will show which tools and blades options your machine has, can it interact with your selected machine material or not. You can say that all the versatility of your machine and its crazy great craftiness happens right here. This is where you choose and tell your machine what you want, print and then cut, draw a line, score a line or cut a line.

Note: Keep in mind that its different options depend on Machine selection (Maker, Explore, or Joy). See below that which options every machine has.

1.2.1. Cricut Explore

If you are working with the Explore machine, then "linetype" option has layers of possibilities for getting results. These options will direct your device, which tool to use. Right now, there are four options (Cut, Draw, Score, and Foil). These four options also link to the next colored box, which Cricut experts called it "Linetype swatch". Linetype swatch availability dependents upon the Cut, Draw, Score, and Foil. Basically, you can say that it used for coloring the image.

1.2.1.1.Cut

If you are choosing cut, then it will direct the machine to use a blade for cutting because its user wants to cut this pattern. "Cut" is the default line type that all of the elements on canvas have; this means that when you press "MAKE IT", your machine will cut those designs.

1.2.1.2. Draw

This option will draw the pattern with a pen. The first thing it will do is not cut the piece of heart; it will draw the design with a pen on the paper which you are using on the Mat.

1.2.1.3. Score

This layer will be scored with a Score. In Explore machine there is only Stylus Scoring option works. The score is a more potent option of the line type. When you assign this attribute to a layer, all of the designs will appear in dashed and scoring not have any linetype swatch attribute. When you have a scoring opting ON, then when you will click on Make it, Cricut neither cut it nor draw, but it will make a pressed sketch of that layer.

1.2.1.4. Foil

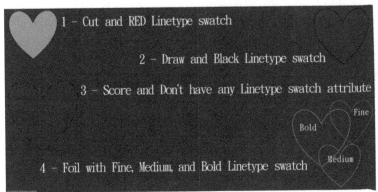

1 – Cut and RED Linetype swatch

2 – Draw and Black Linetype swatch

3 – Score and Don't have any Linetype swatch attribute

Fine

Bold

Medium

4 – Foil with Fine, Medium, and Bold Linetype swatch

Foil option is used to make beautiful foil finishes on projects, and it is primarily working with Foil Paper. It has three further in-depth options, **Fine, Medium,** and **Bold** to do shimmering floral projects, festive cards and invites. Fine, Medium and Bold shows its thickness. Foil has same linetype swatch option as the Cut. See sample of all linetype option of the heart below.

1.2.2. Cricut Maker

Now we are turning to another Machine option "Maker" to understand how the linetype option works in the Cricut Maker. In "Cricut Maker" linetype has 8 options (Cut, Draw, Score, Engrave, Deboss, Wave, Perf, and Foil) and last one Foil as like the Explore has 3 more options (Fine, Medium, and Bold).

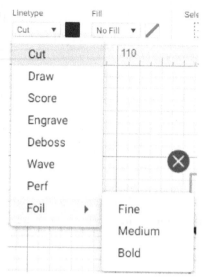

Cut, Draw, Score, and Foil work same in Maker as like in Explore, so I don't talk about them in Maker. Here we will talk about other options which are Engrave, Deboss, Wave, and Perf.

1.2.2.1. Engrave

Engrave means cut or carve a text or design on hard material like creating monograms on aluminum sheets or anodizing aluminum to reveal the silver beneath. Use Engrave to carve unique and permanent designs on materials. Engrave don't work with any linetype swatch.

It works with several materials, Acetate, Aluminum Sheets (0.5 mm), Faux Leather (Paper Thin), Foil Acetate, Foil Holographic Kraft Board – Neon, Foil Poster Board, Garment Leather 2-3 oz. (0.8 mm), Genuine Leather, Glitter Cardstock, Heavy Watercolor Paper – 140 lb. (300 gsm), Kraft Board, Metal – 40 gauge thin copper, Metallic Leather, Metallic Poster Board, Shimmer Paper, Sparkle Paper, Tooling Leather 2-3 oz. (0.8 mm), Tooling Leather 4-5 oz. (1.6 mm), Tooling Leather 6-7 oz. (2.4 mm), Transparency and Vinyl Record.

1.2.2.2. Deboss

This tip will push the material inward like uses a plate to stamp the graphic into the material. In Deboss Linetype swape settings is not enabled. Many materials have been tested by the company which work wonderfully with the Debossing Tool. Its material compatibility list given below.

Adhesive Sheet	Construction Paper	Copy Paper – 20 lb.

Double-Sided		(75 gsm)
Deluxe Paper	Duct Tape Sheet	Faux Leather (Paper Thin)
Flocked Paper	Foil Acetate	Craft Foam
Foil Holographic Kraft Board - Neon	Copy Paper – 32 lb.	Foil Poster Board
Freezer Paper	Genuine Leather	Glitter Cardstock
Glitter Craft Foam	Heavy Cardstock – 100 lb.	Heavy Chipboard
Medium Cardstock – 80 lb. (216 gsm)	Kraft Board	Light Cardstock – 60 lb. (163 gsm)
Heavy Watercolor Paper – 140 lb. (300 gsm)	Kraft Cardstock	Light Chipboard – 0.37 mm
Light Glitter Paper	Light Patterned Paper	Matboard
Metallic Poster Board	Mulberry Paper	Pearl Paper
Poster Board	Shimmer Paper	Sparkle Paper
Sticker Paper - Removable	Sticky Note	Tooling Leather 2-3 oz. (0.8 mm)
Tooling Leather 4-5-oz. (1.6 mm)	Tooling Leather 6-7 oz. (2.4 mm)	Transparency and Vellum

1.2.2.3. Wave

Instead of cutting straight lines like the fine point blade, Wavy Blade creates wavy effects on final cuts. Getting curved lines in Design Space is quite complicated, so this tool will come in handy if you like these sorts of products. It uses to add a whimsical wavy edge to any design and do this in half the time of a drag blade. It can be used for decals, envelopes, cards, gift tags, and collage projects, or any time. The Linetype swape settings are enabled so you can change its color. Again, there is a long list of material compatibility.

Note: Keep in mind whatever machine you're working with, only those materials will be qualified for the use which will be selectable. Any option which turned into a light grey color will show not compatible with selected Machine material.

Adhesive Foil, Matte	Construction Paper	Copy Paper – 20 lb. (75 gsm)
Copy paper – 24lb	Printable Vinyl	Faux Leather (Paper

		Thin)
Foil Acetate	Acetate	Craft Foam
Cotton, Bonded	Copy Paper – 32 lb.	Foil Poster Board
True Brushed Paper	Genuine Leather	Glitter Cardstock
Glitter Craft Foam	Glitter Iron-On	Foil Embossed Paper
Medium Cardstock – 80 lb. (216 gsm)	Kraft Board	Light Cardstock – 60 lb. (163 gsm)
Heavy Cardstock – 100 lb.	Kraft Cardstock	Light Chipboard – 0.37 mm
Washi Sheet	Light Patterned Paper	Sticker Paper
Metallic Poster Board	Sparkle Paper	Pearl Paper
Poster Board	Shimmer Paper	Sparkle Paper
Sticker Paper	SportFlex Iron-On	Printable Fabric
Fleece/Plush	Felt, Craft, Stiff, wool fabric	Flannel
Bubble Holographic Vinyl	Cardstock, Adhesive-Backed Glitter	Cotton
Crepe Paper – Fine	Crepe Paper – Extra Fine	Duct Tape Sheet
Everyday Iron-On	Foil Holographic Kraft Board – Neon	Foil Iron-On
Fusible Fabric	Glitter Mesh Iron-On	Heavy Watercolor Paper – 140 lb.
Holographic Iron-On	Holographic Mosaic Iron-On	Holographic Sparkle Mosaic Iron-On
Holographic Threads Vinyl	Linen	Metallic Iron-On
Metallic Leather	Pearl Metallic Vinyl	Patterned Iron-On
Pearl Metallic Vinyl	Photo Paper	Polyester

1.2.2.4. Perf

Perf is the abbreviation of Perforation. This tool creates evenly spaced perforation lines allowing for clean. It will enable you to cut your materials in small and uniform lines to create perfect and crisp tear effects. You are even tearing without the need to fold beforehand, like the ones you see in raffle tickets, coupons, tear-out cards, especially great for shapes with curves etc. The other swape option of linetype not enabled in perf.

1.2.3. Cricut Joy

Now the last machine is "Cricut Joy". This machine material is not working with all linetype options and also with swape options. There are only two linetype options enable that are Cut and Draw, furthermore both of them are enabled for linetype swape.

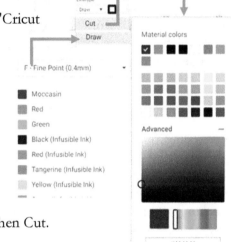

1.3. Fill

Use to select a color or pattern to fill your image layer for Print then Cut.

1.3.1. Print

This option first prints the design by your printer then go on to cut. It enables when the Cut Linetype is selected. This option only works with "Cricut Explore" and "Cricut Maker" with the condition, that filetype option is on the "Cut" option but it's not work in "Joy Machine" even with Cut linetype.

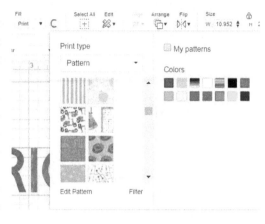

1.3.2. No Fill

The other one "No Fill" means that you won't be printing anything. See in the screenshot in which the linetype option "Cut" is by default working, and in the next "Fill" option "Print" option is available which has 2 more (Color and Pattern) options. It's an excellent option get a Print in Patterns. You can also add your own pattern to pretty much any kind of layer. That's why we say the imagination with Cricut is your limit!

1.4. Select All

If you want to move duplicate, attach, group, cut, copy and paste to all the layers then use select all option.

1.5. Edit

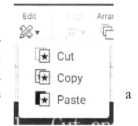

The 5th tool is "Edit". You can use this drop-down option to Cut, Copy and Paste layers or images. Cut and Copy tools activate when you select an element on the canvas. There is little difference between Cut and Copy.

Cut means remove the image from the current place and paste it to another.

Copy means image remain at the current location and can duplicate it. But the **Paste** option will be enabled when you have copied or cut something.

1.6. Align

If the Align Tools are new for you, then let me tell you the Align Menu is master to perfection. It sets the margin that aligns two or more objects. If you have layers of items, then you have to things line up to the left, right, top, or bottom, or have horizontal or vertical centers. It can also distribute objects evenly vertically or horizontally. You may have experienced all these tools with other graphic design programs or in MS Office, most likely you'll know how to use these tools.

Align has two options "Align" and "Distribute". Furthermore, align has seven alignments and distribute two distributions. They help build intricate designs.

1.6.1. Align

1.6.1.1. Align Left
When using this setting, it will set two or more objects to the left margin. The furthest element of the left will dictate, and the margin will take on the left-most edge of your left-most item.

1.6.1.2. Center Horizontally
It will set two or more selected objects in a column and line them up by their center point rather than top or bottom. The central point will take all selected items to the exact horizontal center.

1.6.1.3. Align Right
When using this setting, it will set two or more objects to the right margin. The furthest element of the right will dictate, and the margin will take on the right-most edge of your right-most item.

1.6.1.4. Align Top
It defines the top margin of objects. The selected elements will all be aligned by their top-most edge of your top-most item.

1.6.1.5. Center Vertically
Same like "Center Horizontally", the central point will take all selected objects to the exact vertical center. It will align all your selected items in a row and line them up by their center instead of right or left.

1.6.1.6. Align Bottom

It defines the bottom margin of selected objects. The margin will take all selected items on the bottom-most edge of your bottom-most object.

1.6.1.7. Center

It will move all selected images and stacked them on top of each other. This will exact central point by vertical, horizontal, top and bottom, that's why all pictures will be upon each other.

1.6.2. Distribute

Distribute arrange the elements with equal spacing is a very time-consuming task, and it's not 100% right. So, by distribution option, you can space out objects with the perfect equal amount of distance.

1.6.2.1. Distribute Horizontally

It will move selected images, so they are spaced along a horizontal line between the left and right edges of the selection. The furthest object on the left and the most distant object on the right will determine the spacing. All other items will be placed evenly within the middle.

1.6.2.2. Distribute Vertically

It will move selected images, so they are spaced along a vertical line evenly between the top and bottom edges of the selection. The furthest object on the top and the most distant object on the bottom will determine the spacing. All other items will be placed evenly between two.

1.7. Arrange

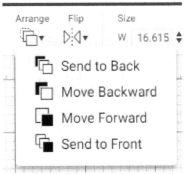

When work with multiple images, text, and designs, always every new creation appears in front of everything. However, any of the elements of your design need to be on the second point below the front, and some need to be set as background at last. Then change the order of objects appear on the Canvas, with "Move to Back", "Move Backward", "Move to Front", and "Move Forward". Changes will be reflected in the Right Panel or Layers Panel.

1.7.1. Send to Back

It will send the selected object to the back at the last point. You will see the item appear at the bottom of the Layers Panel, which is also Right Panel in our example.

Suppose that you have placed four objects on each other. You select the second one and send it to back, and the chosen item will go at the bottom of all four things.

1.7.2. Move Backward

It will send the selected object to one layer's backwards. You will see the item appear one layer lower on the Layers Panel.

Let's understand with an example, suppose again, you have drawn four objects upon each other, but now you want front item go one step back to the front. Now select that element which you want to send one step back and select "Move Backward" from the popup menu.

1.7.3. Move Forward

It will move the selected object one layer up or forward. After this menu selection, you will the object appear one layer higher in the Layers Panel.

Suppose, you have drawn four objects upon each other, but now you want last item (which is currently at the previous point) come one step up (Means at the third point). Now select that element which you want to send one step up and select "Move Forward" from the popup menu.

1.7.4. Send to Front

It will send the selected object to the front of all items. You can also notice the item will appear at the top of the Layers Panel.

Now understand it again, you already have drawn four objects on the Canvas. Now you want to bring last one, or second last, or anyone from behind, to the front select that item and click on the "Send to Front" option from the popup menu.

1.8. Flip

Flip is used for changing directions an object horizontally or vertically. If you are making such design which needs to make a reflection or need the opposite direction or a shadow, this is great way.

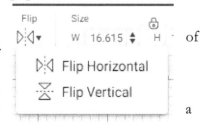

1.8.1. Flip Horizontal

This will Flip an object horizontally. Use it for reflection of image or design horizontally. It works like a mirror; It's handy when you are trying to create wings, heart, legs or any cartoon, especially for those items which have left and right same design.

1.8.2. Flip Vertical

This will Flip an object vertically. It's kind of you sees your reflection in the water. Or any mirror placed on the earth and you are watching in by bent on it. Its work's better for making a shadow.

1.9. Size

Size   🔒

W   11.252 ⬍   H   10.952 ⬍

Everything we create or type whether in Cricut Design Space or any other app has a size. You can change the length from the element by tiny Arrows. When you click on the upper arrow, it increases the height or width, and by clicking on down key, you can decrease your design size. However, if you need an item to have an exact measurement, then type your own desired height or width in these boxes.

There is also something essential, which is a tiny lock. When you increase or decrease the size of an image, the proportions are always locked. By clicking on the small safety, you can change the dimensions.

1.10. Rotate

If you want to set any particular angle in your design, then use Rotate option. You can adjust any exact angle of your object by typing or use the arrows to adjust the angle, and it always set 1 degree at a time. Its maximum degree is 359 degree and minimum 0.

1.11. Position

It is used for adjusting the position of the object from the top left corner of the Canvas. When you click on a specific design, it will show you where your items are on the canvas area.

2. Text Editing

The Text Edit tool is another editing tool in the top panel, but it will appear when you enter any text box in Cricut Design Space canvas. Text editing works very similarly to the Image Editing tool like sizing, rotating and positioning text. It also makes finding the best font and editing text so you can easily personalize your projects. The box which appears around your text when it is selected called a bounding box.

Learn below in simple steps how to easily manipulate and edit the text in Cricut Design Space Canvas.

2.1. Font

Design Space makes it easy to customize your project using text and different fonts. You can use Cricut fonts as well as any system font installed on your computer, iOS device, or Android device.

When you add a text box, this text editing will enable you to click on this panel, and you can select any font for your projects. By clicking on the text box, you can see a little box on the top of the window will appear search for fonts in the fonts box.

If you have the subscription of Cricut Access, you can use any of the fonts within the design space. There are three options for choosing fonts All, system, and Cricut. System fonts are free to use, and Cricut fonts are paid by Cricut access. So, if you don't have to buy Cricut access, use system's fonts.

2.2. Style

Once you have written your text, you have the option to change its form after fonts.

Some of the options you have:

Regular: This is a by default setting, and it won't change the style of your font.

Bold: It will make the font thicker.

Italic: It will little bend (tilt) the font to the right.

Bold italic: You can use this option for both of two type text styling thicker and tilt to the right.

2.3. Font Size, Letter & Line Space

You can't imagine how AMAZING these options are.

Font Size: If you want to change the font size manually, then use this option. And also, can adjust the size of your fonts from the canvas area.

Letter Space: Every font has its letter spacing, and some fonts have less gap and some more between each letter. This option allows for reducing the space between letters very quickly. It's seriously a game-changer.

Line Space To giving space between lines, then this option will handle it in a paragraph; this is very useful. After all, sometimes, I am forced to create a single line of text because I am not happy with the spacing between lines.

2.4. Alignment

Text Alignment differs from the shapes or objects "alignment". This option is for paragraphs.

These are the options you have:

Left: Align a paragraph to the left

Center: Align a paragraph to the center

Right: Align a paragraph to the right.

2.5. Curve

This option will turn your text into extra creativity. This option is best for moving text around any circle; with this function, you can change the diameter of text. The best way to learn it's by moving the slider to left and right. Select your text, when you move the slider to the left, it will turn the text upwards as like you are drawing a circle from page bottom to top; and when you move the slider to the right, it will bend the text from a straight line to downwards.

Note: To make a complete circle, move the slider entirely to the left, or right.

2.6. Advance

Advance is the last option on the writing editing panel. Don't be panic by seeing the name of this drop-down menu. Once you know the use of all the options, you will see they are not that hard to understand.

Ungroup to Letters

This option is used to separate each letter into a single word selection. Before applying this option, you will see when you click on the text box entire box will be selected and you can't change the font of a single word, but after ungrouping, you can choose every single word and change fonts.

Ungroup to Lines

As like the ungroup letter, this option is to allow you to separate a paragraph on individual lines. Type your section, then click on ungroup to lines and there you have it; a separate line that you can now modify.

Ungroup to Layers

Ungroup to layers is the trickiest of all of text ungrouping options. This option only works for Multi-Layer fonts; these kinds of fonts are only available after purchasing and, or Cricut Access. A multi-layer font is a type of font that has a condition like 3D. These fonts are used for making shadow or color around the text.

IF you have a font that is multi-layer and you want to edit these layers, select the text box and click on ungroup to layers to separate every single layer.

3. Left Panel Orange – Insert Area

With the top panel about which we also divide it into three parts Title bar, Image Editing bar, and Text editing Bar. We explained it in detail so now we are going to edit all of the designs—changing shapes, inserting text, uploading own images, using Cricut projects, and inserting built-it Cricut templates.

This left panel has seven options for designing.

3.1. New

It is used to create a new project in the canvas area. When you are going to designing then go to new option a new canvas paper will open. Start your work here. Suppose you are already working on any projects. A warning message will appear at the top of the canvas and remind you to save the previous file or replace it—check option you want to keep it for next time or cancel it to continue the current project.

3.2. Templates

Remember first that the feature is working only in desktop software. Android and iOS app do not have this essential function.

Templates will help you for visualizing how looks your design on the Cloth, Mug, Necklace, Shirt, bags, banners and so on. This feature is just for a preview, it will not save in your project, and not even cut.

3.3. Projects

If you don't have time, or not want to make itself or like's any other project but just want to do some little bit changes, then this feature is best for you.

- Go to the project.
- Filter your desired project.
- Tap on it. When the project opens, its details will be shown, click below on "Make It" if you don't want to make any changes, and "customize" for doing some changes.

Remember that you can only cut those projects which are labelled free otherwise need to purchase Cricut Access membership.

3.4. Images

As we told previous, there are thousands of images, so you can use them in your project to give them a celebrity reputation. There is also an option of searching and filter to find your desired image easily. Some possibilities with keywords are also given Highlighted Categories, Themes, people and places, Occasions, Shapes, and trending, they also have many subcategories.

Cartridges have many other cartoon characters-based images which you to purchase separately. Sometimes it comes with Cricut Access package sometime not.

3.5. Text

As we talked about it in Text editing, it's a box for writing. Whenever you want to write just click on it, write your words and drag it anywhere on the Canvas.

3.6. Shapes

Use shapes for creating any other shape. With shapes option, you can create simple and less complicated shapes.

There're ten shapes you can choose from:

- Triangle
- Pentagon
- Hexagon
- Star
- Octagon
- Heart
- Circle
- Diamond
- Line
- Square

The line is used as a score line to create fold and score. It used for making Cards and box.

3.7. Upload

And the last option or feature in Left panel is upload. That's the exciting option you can upload here your photoshop images, or from internet project images and patterns. Patterns we talked in previous paragraphs are used for print image filling.

4. Right Panel Blue – Layers Area

Design Space has many tools for designing and to customize projects or your images. The Layers panel has four features at the top of the panel and five at the bottom to make a Group, Ungroup, Duplicate, Delete, Slice, Weld, Attach, Flatten and Contour.

The layer is every single element or design that you draw on the canvas area.

Think like wearing winter clothing; when you dressed up in winter, you have multiple layers, that warm you and you get a proper outfit. Also, something happens with a design; stairs of layers depending on the complexity of the project, a complex project has different types of coatings that'll make up the entire project.

For example, see in the image, there are four hearts, one text box, and wings behind the hearts. It means the project has five layers. Hearts are grouped because I want to drag them on the Canvas freely and don't want to destroy its settings red at the bottom, yellow at the second point, again red and then yellow.

Now see in the layers panel, I write text at first, but it is on the front because I use a arrange option here and place it on the front. In layers panel text shows it is on the front, and wings show they are at last on the canvas so also can see at the latest on the layers panel.

You can only modify those images and designs which has layers. If you upload PNG or JPEG, then remember such type of images, projects, or items will not change.

4.1. Group/Ungroup

You can use it for Grouping multiple layers, images, or text together so that they move and size together. These settings will do your complex project too much easy. When you want to move things around the canvas area, so understand them and make friends with them. Group of images or layers will not affect how images are laid out on the cutting mats.

Ungroup is using to separate all layers, images, or text so you can move them freely and size them independently. For text, select "Ungroup" once allows you to move and resize each layer of text independently. Selecting "Ungroup" for a single box which is also you can call a layer of text will allow you to move and resize each letter of text freely. Its work same for as like we talk in previous text editing part.

4.2. Duplicate

If you don't want to do copy and paste separately, then use this duplicate option. Its option work same as copy-pasting but in one step.

4.3. Delete

Delete option is used for removing image, text or objects.

4.4.Slice

This word itself explains its own meaning. Slice means pieces, and you can use it for splitting two overlapping layers into a separate part. Suppose design space doesn't have half-circle, circle in four parts, or ring but you need it in your design then use square and circle together and apply slice option, the circle will cut into pieces.

1. Select a square and circle shape from the left panel and draw on the

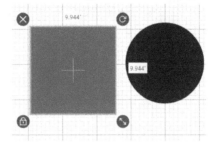

Canvas.

2. Place the square box in the midpoint of circle. select both shapes together and select slice option from the right panel.

3. See in the image below circle cut into two pieces and square portion also cut with it.

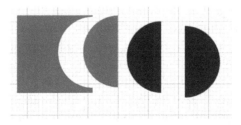

4. Repeat steps again and cut half circle into more pieces.

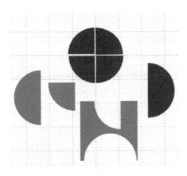

4.5. Weld

What will come in mind when someone says weld it? To you think that we are welding iron in Cricut space, oh come on you catch it!

Weld has the same meaning also in design space. Use to join multiple layers together and create a new object. It will remove any overlapping lines in layers.

4.6. Attach/Detach

Attach is used to hold your objects in position. So, you can use "Attach" for items to appear exactly on the cutting mat as you arrange them on Canvas.

Use attach option to fasten the draw or score layer to a cut layer to tell the machine where placed text or score line. Detach separates attached layers to cut, draw, or score independently from all other layers.

4.7. Flatten/Unflatten

Give extra support to turn the image into a Printable image with Flatten. Flatten all selected layers into a single layer. Suppose you change the fill from no fill to print, and it will apply to just one layer. But will you do this with every layer one by one? Don't be worry you can do this in one step, select the layers you want to print together as a whole, and then click on flatten. If you don't want it in the single printable image then unflatten it, it will separate all photos.

4.8. Contour

Last option on the right panel's layers tab is Contour. The counter is used to hide any layer from the image.

Suppose you take a project from the projects option. Now is this messy for your project but closely related to your project. Are you worried about how to use and modify it, apply Contour?

Look below an example.

1. Click on the project option from the left panel.
2. Choose the project or image and insert it on the canvas.

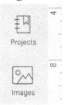

3. Select the image you will see the contour option is still not working. Because Contour option is working with last final image, but this example has layers of design. So, you first need to ungroup the design. Branches aren't grouped so simply drag them away.

4. Now select the highlighted design again and ungroup it. You will see now every layer will be moved freely.

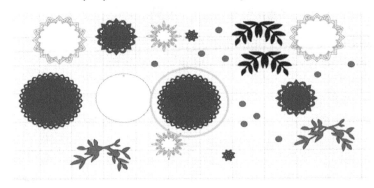

5. Select any one layer in which you want to make changes or want to hide any design. After selection you will see the Contour option will start working. In this example I select the highlighted design.

6. A new file will open now select which part you want to hide. Or don't want to include in your design. After contour the small parts or whole will be hide from your design.

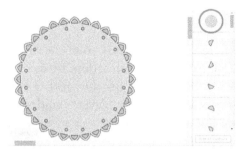

7. Now see in pictures I hide the circle from the center and output is so simple. Now if you want it then delete all extra material from the canvas and cut it by clicking on the "Make it".

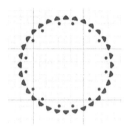

8. Now insert your blade in the Maker machine clamp A and cut your design.

4.9. Visible/Hidden Layer

The eye in the right panel on every design layer indicates that the layer is visible on the Canvas. And what the linetype cut, draw, score, or print you select for making your design. Click on the eyeball icon to hide the selected layer, if you don't want to cut it with your other plan.

4.10.   Color Sync

The last option of the layers panel is color Sync. It will show every color from the canvas area which you used in your image. If your design has multiple shades and doesn't understand good or not, then use this option. If you don't want numerous colors, want to give them one color, drag the design and drop it in the line which color you want to give it.

5. Canvas Area

The canvas area is where you show all of your creativity and see all of your designs and elements. It's very effortless to use! Now, this is your playing ground with boundaries of the grid, zooms security guards, and the editing tools are like your players, guide them on how to play and where to play and win the match as captain of Cricut design space.

Grid is used to divide the canvas area; because every little square you see on the grid helps you to imagine the cutting mat. The measurements can change from inches to cm. You can also hide the grids from the Canvas by click in the corner of the top right of Canvas between two zero.

5.1. Zoom In/ Zoom Out

You have a problem of watching little pieces of design on Canvas. Dare it! Use Zoom in for design neat and clear. By using zoom in the option, you can examine every little corner of your design. When you have done zoom out to original size and look how it looks now nice, Hun...

Are you admiring this effort that we give you a complete visit of Cricut Canvas Ground, Oh thanks for this appreciation? But you know this is not a last ball in the Design Space Ground. It's like a test match, so be ready for the next game which will be played in the next chapter and   Final   in   the   Cricut   Project   Book.

4 Chapter

How To Upload Own Font, Image or Text?

Plan with your Favorite Applications and Use PDF as the Bridge. Would you like to utilize PDF in Cricut Design Space? Regardless of whether you don't have any acquaintance with it yet, you will need to! PDF records can be made in any application. It's a rich vector design that scales to any estimate without losing quality. It's going to turn into your closest companion.

Make your best show-stoppers in any application and spare them as PDF—pdf to SVG changes over them faultlessly to SVG or DXF, prepared for cutting. You'll get an ideal match: no textual style bungles, no wrecked lines, no issues. Invest your energy making in the program that is generally agreeable for you.

The most effective method to utilize PDF in Cricut Cutting Machines

PDF is a vector design. This implies that all the items and text can be exclusively controlled in Cricut Design Space. If you look for counsel on utilizing PDF in Cricut Design Space, you'll be prompted that everything you can do is make a JPEG or PNG picture design. This isn't accurate.

Raster designs are restricted since they are level bitmap pictures. Preferably, since PDF begins as a vector design, you need to change it over to a vector design. This guarantees that no items or text are lost or straightened into raster pictures. Pick a vector design – SVG or DXF. Both are adaptable vector illustrations, ideal for cutting applications. With admittance to the entirety of the articles, qualities, and text, you'll have full authority over each component in your undertaking. I write steps below how I make a small sample in Canva and upload it in Design Space.

- **Utilize Any Vector Drawing Program to Save Your Design as PDF**

You can utilize any attracting or designing app to make your plan. This incorporates straightforward, yet unique assets like Microsoft PowerPoint, Adobe Spark, and Adobe Illustrator Draw for iPad, or Canva which I used in this example. You can even utilize the drawing and clipart apparatuses in Microsoft Word! However long it is a vector drawing program and can spare or share a PDF document, and you are good to go. You'll have the option to utilize your PDF in Cricut Design Space.

- **Save in PDF and Convert from PDF to SVG or DXF**

I use moon vector, stars vector and tree from the Canva library and save them as PDF file. Whenever you have made your PDF document, convert it by using Google. Pick SVG or DXF as the yield design. SVG is better and quicker for most plans. DXF can be used if the drawing is too unpredictable. Either design gives you an incredible way to utilize PDF in Cricut.

- **Transfer your Design to Cricut Design Space**

Select Upload option from the left panel in Design Space to add your image which you converted over SVG or DXF document to the library. Click on the "Upload image) and Insert your saved Image to open it on your plan board.

Image

Upload your images for free (basic and vector).

Images can be .jpg, .gif, .png, .bmp, .svg, or .dxf files

Upload Image

uploaded images   View All

Presently you have your PDF in Cricut's organization! Now give it to

any name.

Now select your image from library and click on the "Insert images" button to insert image on the design space Canvas.

- **Calibrate Your Design**

Since you've figured out how to utilize PDF in Cricut Design Space, you are prepared to will work! When the drawing shows up on-screen, you'll have the option to alter all items, characteristics, and text. On the right, you'll see the entirety of the components recorded. You would now be able to utilize all the recognizable highlights to conceal objects,

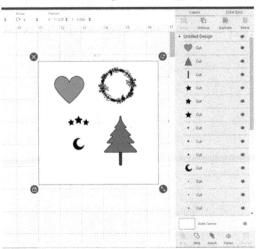

change credits and tweak situating.

If you used a program that supports gatherings or layers, these would show up also.

Illustration of PDF changed over to SVG and afterwards brought into Cricut Design Space.

For what reason is PDF being a Great Design Choice for Cricut Devices?

Masterful Freedom. By picking PDF as your yield design, you can utilize any coaxing programming out there, on any gadget. Indeed, even free applications on iPad like Adobe Illustrator Draw will give you the force you need to make incredible plans. All your instrument of a decision should have the option to do is spare or offer as PDF.

PDF in Cricut implies Flexibility. Since PDF is a vector design, all the imported components in Cricut Design Space will be adaptable. This means that you can resize them from small to tremendous without avoiding a beat.

Change Those Attributes. With Bitmap pictures like PNG and JPEG, what you see is the thing that you get. You can't change tones, and you can't change objects. Everything you can do is turn the entire level picture on or off for cutting. In vector designs like SVG, each component can be moved, changed, erased or resized. Utilizing vector illustrations, you have a lot better degree of power over your show-stopper.

Instances of Vector versus Bitmap in Cricut Design Space

The following are instances of vector and bitmap illustrations in Cricut Design Space. As should be obvious, the vector designs permit you the opportunity to tweak and alter your plan directly in Design Space. Usefulness is exceptionally restricted with bitmap pictures like PNG and JPEG. With these, you can simply determine what's inside and outside the cutting lines. Peruse more about how to utilize vector and raster pictures on the Cricut Help Forum.

At the point when you pick a vector design like SVG or DXF, you have all-out authority over your plan – objects ascribe like tone and revolution, gatherings, layers and what's on or off for cutting. In this model, we've imported the PDF above yet changed the size and position of the moon. If this were a bitmap picture, you would have to in a real sense, return to the planning phase, recover the image and import it once more.

Install Fonts For Cricut Design Space

You can also do the same thing with Fonts. If you like any font from your Canva account then write what you want Like I write "Cricut Design Space" in do different fonts and save the file in PDF. Again, convert it into SVG file. I don't use any specific converter for converting file from PDF to SVG but most of the time I get better result from zamzar, get just by doing simple Google PDF to SVG. When you are using PDF to SVG for fonts then it will also come in layers in design space but it's like an image you can't change text by using this method. But below we also tell you how to download your own fonts for Design Space from third party instead of Cricut Access.

To truly customize all Cricut crafts and projects, you must need fonts. The Cricut Access also has hundreds of fonts, but still, you want to add any other. Then in this part, we guide you on how to upload your own desired fonts to Cricut Design Space! It's easy and gives you free access to other fonts from outside the Cricut Access.

For adding your own font into Design Space, you need to have installed that font in your own system that you can use it in Design Space as system fonts. So first download your targeted font in your desktop and install it in the system. As see blow how I download my fonts, install it and then use it in Design Space.

Note: Before going to install free fonts. I must warn you that you can use only these fonts for your personal use because may some fonts have a copyright issue. If you are planning to use Cricut as starting a business, then you may sell your product online too. There is a hell of copyrighting in the online market, so keep away from the edges of this hell. It's better to buy the membership of the Cricut Access for using other fonts.

There are hundreds of websites from where you can download font. If you have the plan to purchase Fonts, then Fontbundles.net is good and also recommended by other Cricut experts, here you can get free fonts also. The other one for free font downloading is dafont.com, and here you can get free but also can donate to the Author.

One more thing I want to tell you that Cricut cuts according to Mat grid no following means cuts mathematically. Simple files, fonts and projects cut better than complicated. So, fonts which Cricut use are designed mathematically simple, so cutting is better and comfortable than problematic. However, system fonts are also not always straightforward. But the cutting of rough or blush edgy font will not give you good result than of bold and clear edges. It does not happen only with fonts but can also occur with, PNG, JPEG, and GIF if its boundaries are not much clear to adjust the blade and mat direction with every little angle, so it will not be cut clean and clear. The simple thing is to make a sample of that font before going on to the intricate project print and cut.

Let's install the font for it. I am designing my book cover in it with downloaded fonts. Starts by creating a square for the cover front, back and for the spine. Then draw heart, circle, square, triangle, diamond, hexagon, octagon, star and pentagon all the Shapes from the tool in the Design Panel, and resizing them to look good on the page. Enter an image from the "Images" option and then text box.

1. Download your font, and maybe it is in a zip folder. Click on the zip folder by right-click open menu and click extract file. Then a new folder will open with three files in it. One will be license, one Font picture and a font installing the file.

2. Right-click on file which has type "TrueType font" or which is other than text or PNG. Click on "Install" from the right-click menu.

3. After installation opens your Design Space or refreshes it, draw a text box and search for an installed font by name. Now write with your font and decorate your canvas.

5 Chapter

Text Effects

During designing, every creativity needs some special text effects to make the design more relaxed and professional. But you may notice in the design space most of the things not pre-installed or prepared for making such that changes which often we saw in smartphone apps and designing apps. So then what question came mind. Is design space fail in making effects?

The answer is no because, during canvas overview, we talked about the reflections, so it will make it impossible that text effects do not drive in it. It's maybe tricky for some people who don't know the ABC of layers and designing and also use of tools for developing shadow, reflecting or drip effects. But Know in this chapter, we talk about some effects.

How to Create Text Shadow in Cricut Design Space

In text-shadow, I show you how to make the shudder around the word. Currently, Cricut design space not have any Shadow effect which you can use freely. I will tell you in steps or with cheat sheet how to do this by using the same things but with some complex layers.

Offset Text Shadow

1- Open a new project and draw a text box.
2- Enter your text and choose the font which you want to use for it. I choose Embassy BT.

3- Now select the box and ungroup its layers for making some changes in letters space. And group them again.
4- Select box again and duplicate the box. Change the color of one text box and keep it aside. See below in the image.

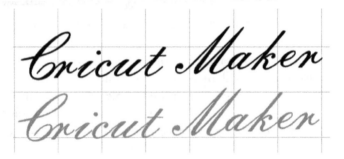

5- Now again duplicate the text box, which is in black. I repeat it eight times.

6- Keep every box over each other to make it a little wider and keep going with each of the remaining layers. Carefully adjust the layers.

4. Now select everything and then go down to the bottom of the Layers panel and click the weld button. So, it welds it together all in one piece.

5. Now pull pink color box below the black layer and select all, go back down to the bottom of the right panel menu and weld it one more time.

Now another type of shadow keeps the pink color over the black and weld it again.

With one picture and text overlapping got minimum 7 result

1. Tap on a new project. Insert "Drip" image from the left panel.
2. Draw a text box, write your words and any font which you want

and place the box over the drip image.

3. Perfectly attach from corners. After corner setting select both boxes to gather and press slice option from right click drop down menu. See below a text and drip image cut will cut into four pieces.

7- Now attach these pieces in multiple ways to create a new style. When group two pieces.

1. When select both pieces and attach them.

8- When First attach then welds them.

9- When First attach then flattens.

10- When just flattens them.

11- Delete extra part from point no 3 image and open contour by selecting drip image and hide all small pieces.

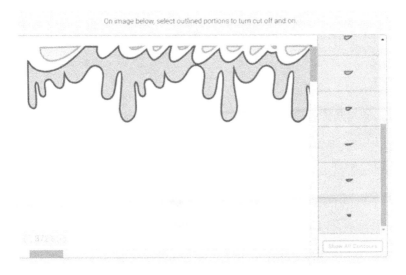

12- Place back text box and drip image. These two results will come out. This is just some ways there are hundreds of ways to make effects.

Conclusion

We wrote this book for those who want to start crafting with Cricut first time. May you hear a lot about the machine and you were so excited to work with. But after buying you faced the problems in understanding and don't know how machine work. Which panel for what purpose, and how to use tools?

We wrote this book according to our problems which we faced when the first time started a collaboration with Design Space. Our less knowledge about machines, especially first-time use of design space surprises us that indeed there is any home used machine which only works with a smart system. But the beauty of success was time. By the time, everyday efforts, and most importantly doing experiments with software shapes, text, images, and projects teach us how to use Design Space.

Now, after giving you a complete overview of Canvas which is the most important and essential in design space, we move to the last but not least step "Projects."

Projects are for doing practice and giving you some ideas to try things some other way. But keep in mind choose that machine, which you will use for final output not happen that you do a project with one machine tools and trying to cut it with others. Use this to make your life, home and those of your friends and family more exciting and beautiful.

Well, now you are in! Learn everything which you need to know about designing your project. This has been an exciting trip into the Cricut Machine world and the various ways in which you can make it work wonders for you.

We have talked about how the design space great tools for mating your most imaginative and creative ideas come to life. Whether you are an avid hobbyist or perhaps looking to take up a new craft, especially if you have some extra time on your hands, then the Cricut Machine offers various means for you to make your wildest ideas come to life.

So, what's the next step? If you are still on the fence about purchasing your very own Cricut machine, then it would be a great idea to do a cursory search online so you can get other users' impressions and opinions about this machine. By reading and hearing about what other users have to say, you can get an idea of just how useful this machine can be for you. Also, do check out the various options in terms of models and pricing that are available to you. If you happen to be unsure about which model works best for you, take a minute to go back to the descriptions we have provided for each of the models. That way, if you are interested in a light machine that is good for less complicated jobs, Joy can work well for you. If you are looking for a heavy-duty machine, then the Maker is what you need, but if you are looking for the best overall value, then the Explore Series can provide you with the features and functions you are looking for.

Additionally, do make a point of checking out blogs and social media where users and designers present their creations. Often, these blogs and social media sites can provide you with the inspiration you need to make your decision. Now keep this part of the book in front of your eyes and create projects. Always start from simple and easy projects. I suggest you first try Cricut access free and simple projects because they also have directions for "Make It" and tell you which material used for the selected design